P9-CDC-482

FUN WITH SCIENCE

LIGHT

BRENDA WALPOLE

Contents

Use the symbols below to help you
identify the three kinds of practical
activities in this book.

EXPERIMENTS

TRICKS

THINGS TO MAKE

Illustrated by Kuo Kang Chen · Peter Bull

Warwick Press
New York/London/Toronto/Sydney
1987

Introduction

Without light from the sun, all life on earth would come to an end. Green plants need sunlight to make food and you and all the other animals on earth depend on plants for food.

This book will help you to discover more about sunlight and the artificial light produced by means of electricity. You can find out why shadows form, how rainbows appear in the sky, how mirrors reflect light, and why lenses make things appear to be larger or smaller.

You can also find out about light and color. Sunlight is made up of several different colors – these are the colors you see in a rainbow. The color of objects around you depends on which colors they reflect back into your eyes. A special layer at the back of your eyes makes it possible for you to see the world in color. Understanding how the eye works has helped scientists to develop machines such as microscopes, telescopes, cameras, and lasers.

As you carry out the experiments in this book, you will be able to answer the questions on these two pages and come to understand how light and color influences the world around you.

This book covers six main topics:
● Light and shadows
● Reflection
● Refraction
● Light and sight
● Light and color
● Light for life; laser light

A blue line (like the one around the edge of these two pages) indicates the start of a new topic.

▲ How do you make patterns like this on a piece of cloth? (page 33)

▼ If you spun these disks, what colors would you see? (page 27)

▼ Why do shadows appear behind objects when light shines on them? (pages 4–5)

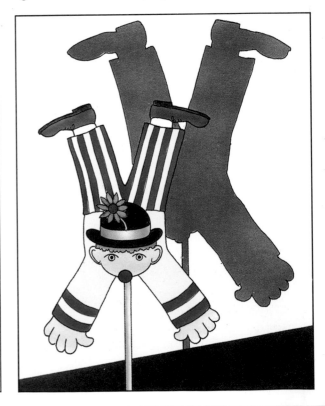

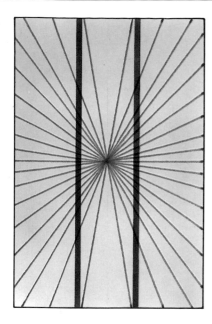

► What makes the colors in a rainbow? (pages 26–27)

▲ Why do these lines appear to be curved, even though they are straight? (page 23)

▼ How does a piece of curved glass make rays of light come closer together? (page 16)

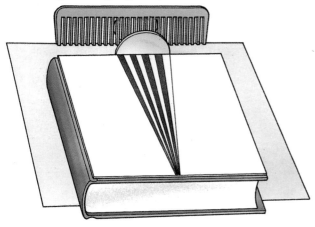

▲ How does a magnifying glass make things look larger? (page 17)

▼ Why can you see reflections in mirrors and other shiny surfaces? (pages 8–9)

▼ Why does grass go yellow if sunlight cannot reach it? (page 34)

Light and Shadows

Light can pass through some substances, such as glass or water. These are called **transparent** and we can see through them. Other substances, such as paper and metal, stop light passing through. They are called **opaque**. Shadows appear behind opaque substances when light shines on them. Shadows are produced because light travels in straight lines and cannot bend around corners. You can see straight lines of light if you look at the rays of light from the sun (right).

Shadow Tricks

Shine a flashlight at a wall in a darkened room. Test a variety of objects and see what sort of shadows they make. See how many different animal shapes you can make using only your hands. You could also draw shadow portraits of your friends or try making up a shadow play using cut-out figures to cast shadows.

Cut out an interesting shape (such as a ship, a plane, or a clown) from a piece of cardboard and fix it to the end of a stick. Try holding the shape close to the light and then further away. What do you notice about the size of the shadow?

Playing with Shadows

On a sunny day, go outside and investigate shadows with your friends. Try drawing around your shadows on a piece of paper and cutting them out. Does your shadow move when you move? Can you jump on your shadow? Can you shake hands with a friend without your shadows touching? What are the biggest and smallest shadows you can make with your body?

Stand in exactly the same place at different times of day and ask a friend to draw around your shadow with chalk. You will find that the position and shape of your shadow changes as the position of the sun changes throughout the day. The shadows made by the sun can be used to tell the time (see pages 6–7).

If the shape is near to the flashlight, it blocks out a lot of light so the shadow is large.

If the shape is further away from the flashlight, it blocks out less light so the shadow is smaller.

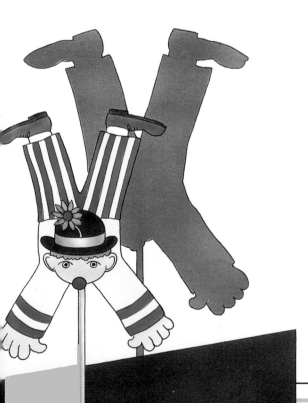

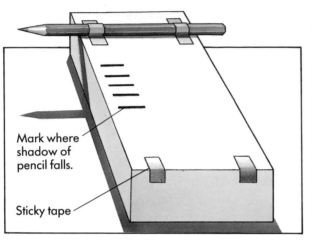

Make a Shadow Clock

Equipment: A long, thin box, pencils, sticky tape, white paper.

Cover one side of the box with white paper and hold it in place with sticky tape. Stick a pencil across the end of the box. On a sunny morning, take your shadow clock outside and place it on a pale-colored, flat surface (such as a sheet of white paper). Point the box in the direction of the sun. Notice where the shadow of the pencil falls and draw a line at the same point on the top of your box. Write the time next to the line. Do this at several different times during the day. At what time is the end of the shadow nearest to the pencil?

Mark where shadow of pencil falls.

Sticky tape

Make a Sundial

To make an accurate sundial, this angle should be the latitude of your town. You can find this in an atlas.

45°

8 inches

6 inches

90°   45°

6 inches

Fold along this line.

Equipment: Thin card, a protractor, a compass, a piece of wood or thick cardboard.

1. On the thin card, draw a right angled triangle. Make the other two angles 45°. The two shorter sides of the triangle should be about 6 inches (15 cm) long. The long side will be a little over 8 inches (20 cm) long.
2. Draw a dotted line as shown in the diagram and cut out the triangle. Fold along the dotted line.
3. Draw a semi-circle on the wood or cardboard as shown in the diagram.
4. Stick the folded part of the triangle firmly to the piece of wood or thick cardboard.
5. Place the sundial in a flat place outside so that the triangle points north-south.
6. Mark the position of the shadow that falls on the base every hour. You should find that the shadow travels the same distance along the semi-circle every hour. On a sunny day you will now be able to tell the time by looking at the position of the shadow on your sundial.

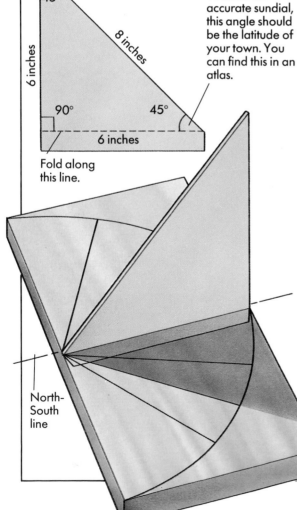

North-South line

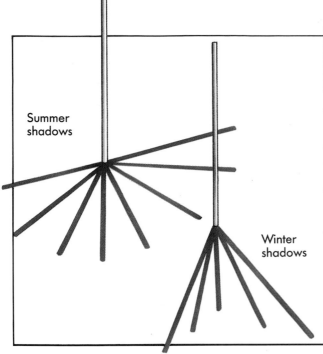

Summer
shadows

Winter
shadows

Shadow Sticks

The shadows made by sticks or poles can be used to investigate the differences between the shadows cast by the sun in winter and summer. Mark the position and length of the shadows made every hour on one day in winter and one day in summer. You can do this with chalk on a hard surface or on a piece of paper placed beside the stick or pole. Make a note of the time next to each line you draw.

- What do you notice about the length of the shadows as the hours go by?
- What differences can you see between summer and winter shadow patterns? Can you see when the days are longest?

Shadows in Space

The moon and the earth cast their own enormous shadows. When the moon passes between the sun and the earth, its shadow falls on parts of the earth. This makes these places dark for a time during the day. This is called an **eclipse** of the sun. When the earth moves between the sun and the moon, it stops sunlight from reaching the moon. The moon becomes dark and this is called an eclipse of the moon.

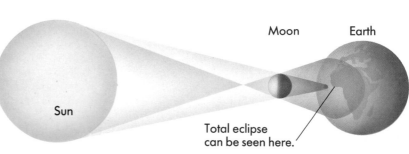

Moon   Earth

Sun

Total eclipse
can be seen here.

▶ Total eclipse of the sun. You can see the faint outer atmosphere of the sun shining out around the black shape of the moon.

Reflections

When rays of light hit a surface or an object they bounce back off again. This is called **reflection**. Look for reflections in foil, cans, bottles, and spoons. You will find that flat, shiny surfaces produce the best reflections. This is why most mirrors are made of flat sheets of highly polished glass with a shiny silver coating behind them. Try the experiments on these two pages to find out more about how mirrors reflect light.

Wave at yourself in a mirror with your left hand. Which hand is your reflection using? Mirrors reverse images so that the left side appears to be the right. Ask a friend to pretend to be your reflection and follow your movements for a while.

Investigate Reflections

1. Cut a hole a piece of the card about 1 inch (2.5 cm) in diameter and tape a comb across the hole.
2. In a darkened room, place the card in front of a flashlight so that narrow beams of light come through the teeth of the comb.
3. Hold a mirror in the beams of light so that it reflects the light.
4. Move the mirror to a different angle. What happens to the beams of light?

You will see the beams more clearly on a dark surface.

Secret Writing

You can write a secret message to a friend using mirror code. Put a piece of paper in front of a mirror. Look in the mirror and carefully write your message on the paper. When you look at the paper, you will see your message back to front in mirror code. Your friend will be able to decode the message by looking in his or her own mirror.

How it works
Light is reflected off the mirror at exactly the same angle as it hits the mirror. When you change the angle of the mirror, the angle of the reflected light rays changes as well.

More and More Reflections

It is possible to see all around an object if you use more than one mirror. This is because the light rays are bounced from one mirror to the other. Stand two mirrors side by side and put a small object between them. How many reflections can you see?

More things to try
● Move the mirrors closer together and then further apart. What happens to the number of reflections?
● Place two mirrors facing each other with an object between them. You should be able to see endless reflections as the light is bounced to and fro between them.

Make a Kaleidoscope

The patterns inside a kaleidoscope are made by light bouncing between the mirrors inside.

Equipment: Three small mirrors (all the same size), sticky tape, card or paper, colored paper shapes or beads.

1. Tape the mirrors together in a triangle.
2. Stand them on the card or paper and draw around their shape.

3. Cut out the triangle of card or paper and tape it to one end of the mirrors.
4. Drop pieces of colored paper or colored beads inside.
5. Look inside your kaleidoscope. How many patterns can you see? Shake the kaleidoscope to change the pattern.

Mirror

Card or paper

Sticky tape

Pattern inside kaleidoscope

Make a Periscope

The commander of a submarine that is below the sea can find out what is happening above the surface by raising a special tube called a **periscope** up out of the water. A periscope uses two mirrors that bounce reflections between them so people can see around corners or look at things that are too high for them to see. You can make a periscope for yourself.

1. Draw three lines on the cardboard to divide it into four equal strips.
2. Cut squares in two of the strips as shown.
3. Cut two lines on each of the other two strips so they make an angle of 45° with the side of the card.
4. Fold the card into a tube shape and stick it together with tape.
5. Slide the mirrors into the angled slits and tape them in position. One mirror should face upward and the other should face downward.
6. If you hold the periscope sideways, you will be able to see around corners. If you hold it upright, you will be able to see over the heads of people or things that are taller than you are.

How it works
Light from the objects that are out of sight is reflected from the top mirror down into the lower mirror. You are able to see the objects by looking in the lower mirror.

Equipment: Two small, square mirrors, a piece of strong cardboard 1 foot × 1 foot (30 cm × 30 cm), sticky tape, ruler, protractor, scissors.

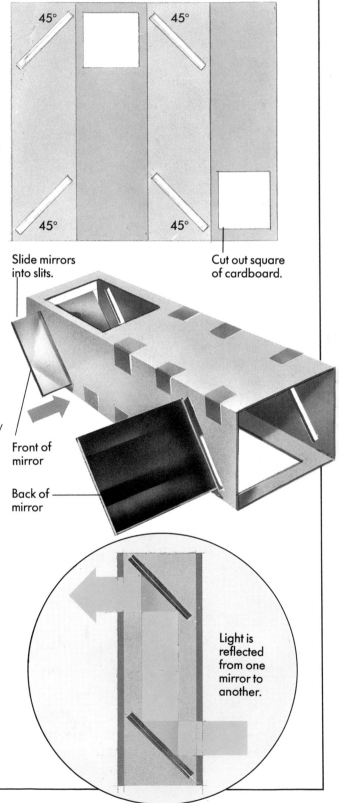

Slide mirrors into slits.

Cut out square of cardboard.

Front of mirror

Back of mirror

Light is reflected from one mirror to another.

Looking at Curved Mirrors

Curved mirrors produce images that are different from those you see in flat mirrors. Look at your face in the front and back of a shiny spoon. How are the images different?

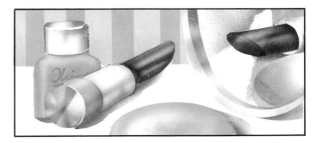

Mirrors that curve outward in the middle (like the back of a spoon) are called **convex** mirrors. They produce an image that is **smaller** than the one you would see in a flat mirror. Convex mirrors are attached to cars. They gather light from a wide area and give drivers a good view of what is happening behind them.

Mirrors that curve inward in the middle (like the front of a spoon) are called **concave** mirrors. They give an image that is **larger** than the one you would see in a flat mirror. Convex mirrors are used for shaving and make-up mirrors. They are also used to make powerful telescopes (see pages 16–17).

► The strange mirrors that you see at some fairgrounds are partly convex and partly concave. Some parts of the reflections are stretched and other parts are squeezed up. People standing in front of mirrors like this look very funny!

Bending Light

Light travels at different speeds through different substances. It travels more slowly through water or glass than it does through air. As the light slows down, it also changes direction a little. This is called **refraction** and it makes the light rays look as if they "bend" at the point where two substances meet.

Water Can Bend Light

Fill a glass with water and place a straw in it. Look down at the straw as it stands in the water. You will see that the straw appears to bend. When you lift the straw out of the water you will see that it is still straight. The light rays change direction when they enter the water and make the straw look as if it bends in the middle. Look at your legs when they are half in and half out of the bathwater and you will see the same effect!

Magic Money

Equipment: A coin, a bowl or cup, water.

1. Put the bowl or cup on a table and place the coin in the bottom.
2. Keep looking at the coin and move slowly backward until the coin disappears from view.
3. Stay standing in the same place and ask a friend to pour water into the cup or bowl. You will find you can see the coin again!

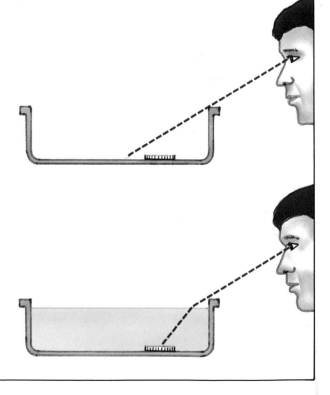

How it works
The light from the coin is "bent" (refracted) by the water so you can see it again. Swimming pools and ponds never look as deep as they really are because light from the bottom is "bent" before it reaches our eyes.

Air Can Bend Light

On a very hot day, you can sometimes see what looks like a pool of water on the road although the road is really completely dry! Light from the sky is "bent" (refracted) by the hot air near the road and the "pool" you see is actually refracted sunlight. This is why people see "mirages" in a desert (see photograph above). The hot air bends the light so objects that are really a long way away appear to be close by.

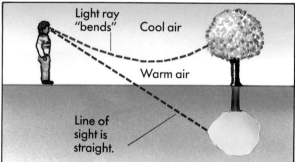

Glass Can Bend Light

Hold a pencil behind a thick glass dish so that half the pencil is above the dish and half is below. You will find that the part of the pencil behind the glass seems to be separated from the part of the pencil in the air. This is because light travels more slowly in glass than in air. The light rays change direction at the edge of the glass and make the pencil look as if it "bends" in the middle.

Glass can be made into different shapes so that it "bends" the light in different directions. Turn over to find out more about this.

Lenses

Transparent materials (such as water or glass), which can bend light rays by refraction, can work as lenses. Lenses are curved on one or both sides and are useful for bending light in special ways. They make objects look larger or smaller, depending on the shape of the lens. You can find out how lenses work on pages 16–17.

Lenses can be made of any clear material that has smooth, clear sides. You have a lens in each eye. People usually make lenses out of glass. They are used in glasses, cameras, microscopes, and telescopes. A microscope (right) uses several sets of lenses and can make tiny objects look hundreds or thousands of times bigger.

Making Things Look Larger...

Water sometimes acts as a lens and makes things look larger. Make a lens from a drop of water to see how this works.

Cut a small hole about 1 inch (2.5 cm) in diameter in a piece of card. Stick a piece of clear tape across the hole. Use a straw to carefully put a drop of water on the tape. Look at a leaf or a page from a newspaper through the drop of water and you will see that the object looks bigger through the lens.

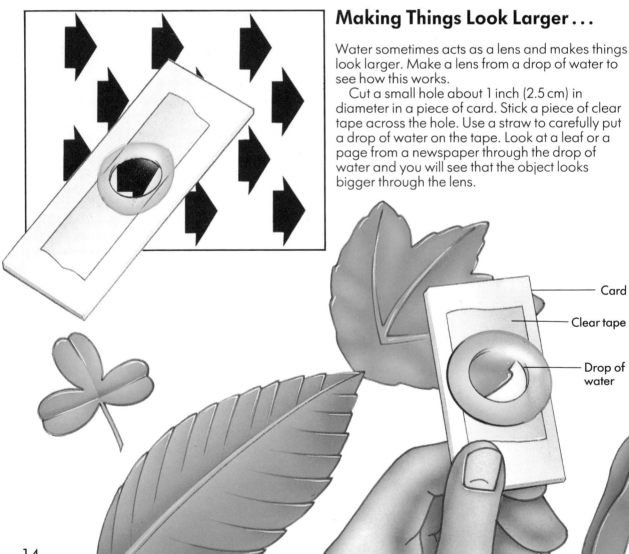

Card

Clear tape

Drop of water

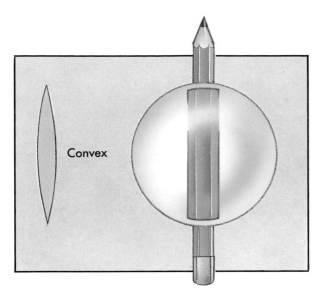

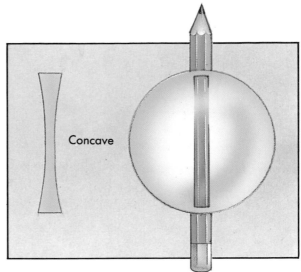

Convex lenses make things look bigger. They are thicker in the middle than they are at the edges so they curve outward. This shape is called convex.

Concave lenses make things look smaller. They are thinner in the middle and thicker at the edges. This shape is called concave.

. . . and Smaller

Ask if you can borrow the glasses of a person who is nearsighted. (He or she finds it difficult to see things that are a long way off.) Try holding the glasses a little way above the print of this page and look through the lens. You will notice that the print looks very tiny.

If you cannot borrow glasses . . . try looking through the bottom of a very thick glass. (This will not work quite as well as the glasses. The letters may be bent out of shape because the glass is not curved exactly.)

How Lenses Work

1. Cut a hole in the card about 1 inch (2.5 cm) in diameter and tape the comb over the hole.
2. In a darkened room, stand the card in front of a beam of light from a flashlight.
3. Lay the white paper in front of the rays of light that come through the comb so you can see them clearly. (You may need to place the paper on top of some books.)
4. Hold the magnifying glass against the edge of the paper and notice what happens to the rays of light.

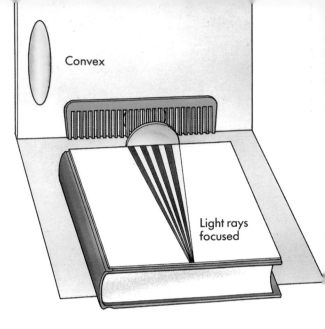

Convex

Light rays focused

Telescopes

One lens held close to a small object can make it look larger but to look at things that are a long way off you need a telescope. Telescopes make things look closer so they can be seen more clearly and studied in detail.

▶ Amateur astronomers use telescopes like this to observe the night sky. This type of telescope reveals details on the surface of the moon and makes it possible to see the rings around Saturn. It can even be used to study galaxies about 50 million light years away.

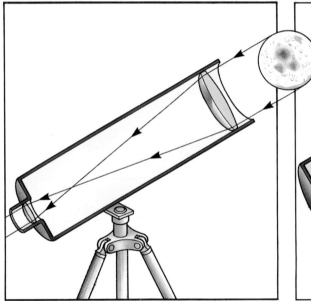

Some telescopes are called **refracting** telescopes because they have two lenses that refract (bend) the light. A large lens collects and focuses the light and a smaller lens makes the image larger so it can be seen clearly.

Other telescopes are called **reflecting** telescopes because they use mirrors to reflect the light. A large, curved mirror reflects the light onto a smaller, flatter mirror which in turn reflects the image onto a small lens. The lens makes the image look larger.

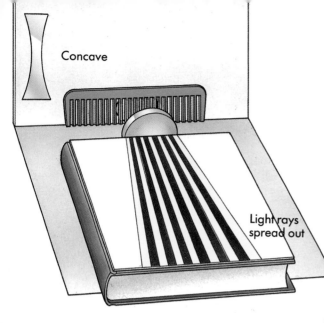

Concave

Light rays spread out

Equipment: A sheet of cardboard, a comb, a flashlight, sticky tape, a magnifying glass, a sheet of white paper, books (optional).

How it works

The magnifying glass is a convex lens. It bends the rays so they all come together at a point. This is called **focusing** the light.

Now repeat the investigation using a concave lens, such as the glasses of a nearsighted person. In this sort of lens the middle of the lens curves inward. This time you will see that the beams of light are spread out instead of being focused.

Make a Telescope

Equipment: A shaving mirror, a small, flat mirror, a magnifying glass.

1. Stand the shaving mirror by a window pointing toward the stars or the moon.
2. Hold the flat mirror so you can see a reflection of the shaving mirror in the middle.
3. Look at the reflection in the flat mirror using the magnifying glass. The stars or moon will look much nearer through the glass lens.

The first reflecting telescope like this was made by Isaac Newton in the mid-17th century.

Warning: Never look directly at the sun (especially through lenses or telescopes). You will damage your eyes.

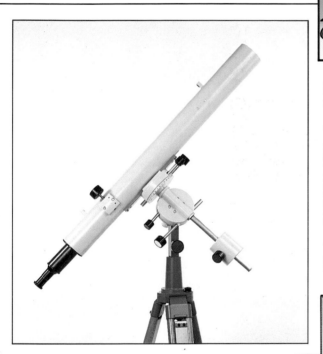

Light and Sight

When your eyes are open, the light reflected from objects around you enters your eyes through the **pupil** – the black hole in the middle. The pupil is an opening in the colored part of the eye, which is called the **iris**. A **lens** behind the eye focuses the light onto a light-sensitive layer called the **retina** at the back of the eye. Special optical nerves carry messages from the retina to the brain, which interprets the images so you can see.

Pupil Power

The pupil in the middle of the eye can change size to control the amount of light entering the eye. You can see this happening if you look closely into your own eyes. Stay in a dimly lit room for several minutes. Look into the mirror and notice the size of your pupils. Then turn on a bright light or move into a brightly lit place and look again at your pupils.

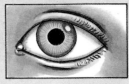

Dark   Light

In dim light, the pupils open wide to let in as much light as possible. In bright light, they become very small to stop too much light from reaching the retina and damaging this sensitive layer.

◄ Cut-away view inside a human eye. The image of the person is upside down because the rays of light travel in straight lines and cross over behind the lens.

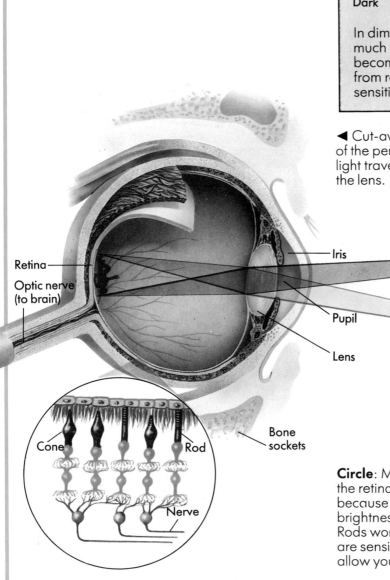
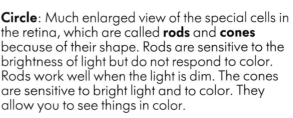

Retina

Optic nerve (to brain)

Iris

Light rays

Pupil

Lens

Cone   Rod

Nerve

Bone sockets

Circle: Much enlarged view of the special cells in the retina, which are called **rods** and **cones** because of their shape. Rods are sensitive to the brightness of light but do not respond to color. Rods work well when the light is dim. The cones are sensitive to bright light and to color. They allow you to see things in color.

Make a Model Eye

Equipment: A round bowl with water inside, black card, white card, a small table lamp without a shade.

1. Make a small hole in the middle of the black card – this represents the pupil in your eye.
2. Place the black card on one side of the bowl and the white card (which represents the retina) on the other side.
3. Place the lamp so it is in line with the two cards and switch on the lamp.
4. Turn off any other lights in the room and pull the drapes (if necessary) to make the room dim.

5. Move the white card to and fro until an image of the lamp appears on it.

How it works
The image you see will be small and upside down. The image that forms on the retina in the back of your eyes is also upside down but your brain is used to this and can interpret the images so you see things the right way up.

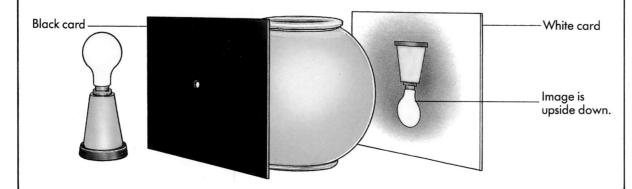

Black card

White card

Image is upside down.

Nearsight and Farsight

Some people cannot focus on things a long way off. This is because the lens in one or both of their eyes focuses the image in **front** of the retina, so the image that forms on the retina is blurred. This is called being **nearsighted** and can be corrected by wearing glasses with concave lenses.

Nearsight

Light rays focus in front of retina.

Farsight

Light rays focus behind retina.

Other people cannot focus on things close to them because the lens forms a clear image **behind** the retina. This is called being **farsighted** and can be corrected with convex lenses.

The Disappearing Rabbit

At the back of the eye is a large nerve (the optic nerve) which leads to the brain. At this part of the retina there are no rods or cones, so if light is focused here you cannot see anything. You will see this effect if you try this trick.

Hold the book up in front of your face at a normal reading distance. Shut your left eye and stare at the magician's wand. Slowly move the book closer to your eye and the rabbit will disappear!

Using Two Eyes

Because you have two images of everything you look at. Each eye looks at the world around you from a slightly different position. This allows you to see things in three dimensions rather than just as a flat picture. It also helps you to judge distances and appreciate perspective.

How Many Pencils?

1. Place a glass of water on a table and stand a pencil about 1 foot (30 cm) behind it.
2. Look through the glass and you will see the images of two pencils in it.
3. Close your left eye and the right hand pencil will disappear. Close your right eye and the left hand pencil will disappear.

How it works
The water is working as a lens to produce the images but because the water is held in a cylinder shape each eye looks through the water at a slightly different angle. So, with both eyes open, you see two pencils. With one eye open you see only one image.

Fly the Rocket to the Moon

Hold the book so your nose touches the dot in the middle of the picture below. Turn the book around slowly in a counterclockwise direction. You should see the rocket fly into space and land on the moon!

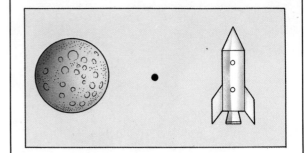

How it works
Each eye sends a slightly different message to the brain. The right eye sees the rocket and the left eye sees the moon. Your brain combines the two pictures and makes the rocket appear to fly.

Touch the Dot

Draw a dot on a piece of paper and put the paper about 2½ feet (75 cm) in front of you on a table. Sit at the table, put a hand in front of one eye and use your other hand to try and touch the dot with a pencil.

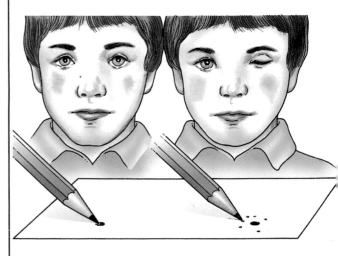

You will find it quite difficult to touch the dot accurately at the first attempt because you cannot judge distances easily with only one eye. You use both eyes to find the exact position of things.

Hole in the Hand

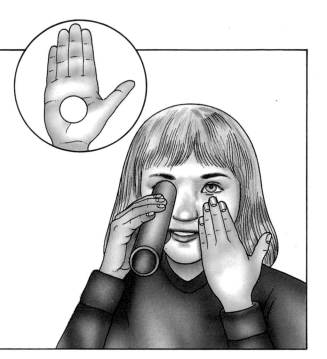

Find a cardboard tube or roll up a piece of paper to make a long tube. Look through the tube with your right eye and hold your left hand up next to the paper with the palm toward you. You should see that there seems to be a hole through the middle of your palm!

How it works
Your right eye sees inside the tube and your left eye sees your open hand. The brain is confused because it receives such different signals from each eye. So it combines the images and you appear to see a hole in your hand.

Make a 3-D Viewer

Equipment: Cardboard, pencil, ruler, scissors.

1. Trace this cross shape onto the card using the pencil and ruler. Make the cross 2 inches (5 cm) high and make each arm of the cross about ½ inch (1.3 cm) wide.
2. Cut out the cross shape to leave a hole in the card.
3. Hold the card upright at right angles to a picture or photograph.
4. Stare hard down through the cross for a few seconds and you should see the picture stand out in three dimensions. (It helps if you **expect** this to happen.)

How it works
The cross shape hides the edges of the picture so you cannot see that it is really flat. Your brain is used to seeing the world in three dimensions and makes the picture **appear** to be three dimensional.

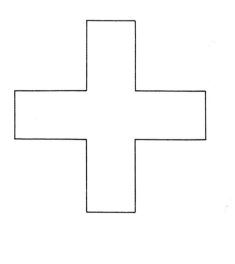

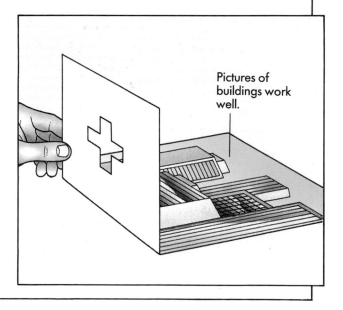

Pictures of buildings work well.

Fool Your Eyes

Here are some tricks to fool your eyes so that objects appear to move when they are really still, and you see objects that are not really there at all! You can also find out how a confusing background changes the shape or size of an object.

See the Ghost in the Castle

Hold this book up in front of you about 1 foot (30 cm) from your eyes. Stare hard at the black ghost and concentrate on its face. Count slowly to thirty. Then immediately look into the archway of the castle. Count to ten and you will see a white ghost appear!

How it works
When you stared at the black ghost, the part of the retina on which the image was formed did not receive any bright light. But the surrounding area worked hard to send back messages to your brain about the bright, white background around the ghost. When you looked at the archway, the area that had formed an image of the

Turn on the Music

Look at this picture of a record on a turntable and move the book slowly around in a circle. Your eyes cannot follow the dark and light stripes round and round because they keep changing their position so quickly. Your brain interprets the picture as a record turning, which is what it **expects** to see.

background was tired and did not respond fully to the white of the archway. This made some of the archway appear slightly gray. But the area of the retina that formed the image of the ghost did work properly and made some of the archway (in the shape of the ghost) appear white. This is why you see a white, ghostly image in the archway.

Confusing Backgrounds

Are all these figures the same size?

Look at these diagrams carefully. The three figures are all the same size but the background lines make the figure on the right appear to be larger than the others. The background pattern in the diagram below confuses the eyes and brain and makes the circle look as if it is not a true circle.

Is this circle round?

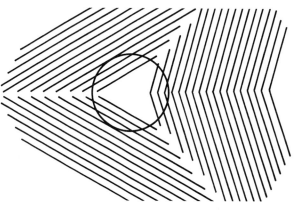

Clues to Size and Distance

Our eyes use many clues from our surroundings to work out how far away things are and how big they are. We often compare the size of things with other objects close by. This gives us a sense of perspective. Look at these examples of pictures that have confusing clues and make it difficult to judge distance and perspective properly.

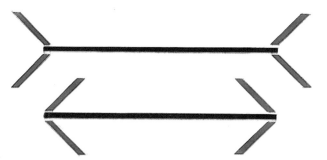

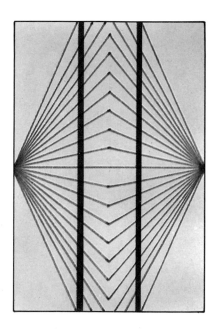

In the diagrams above, the two horizontal lines are the same length but the angle of the arrows makes one line look longer than the other.

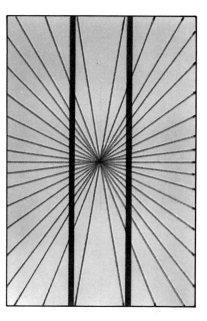

In these two diagrams, the two vertical lines appear to be bent but they are really straight.

Moving Pictures

If your eyes see two pictures very quickly, one after the other, they may not be able to tell that the picture has changed and the image will appear to move. You can only register 12 pictures a second as separate images. If the pictures appear more quickly than this, you see them as moving pictures. Motion pictures have 24 photographs (frames) every second.

How to Make Pictures Move

Before motion pictures were invented, people produced moving pictures using a set of drawings. Each one was slightly different from the one before. The drawings were made into a book, which was flicked quickly with a thumb. This made the pictures appear quickly one after the other so the eyes saw a steady movement. You can try this for yourself, first with just two pictures then with a whole series.

Put the Fish in the Bowl

1. Draw a fish and a bowl separately on a piece of card. Put the fish on one side of the card and the bowl on the other.
2. Fix the card to a thin rod or pencil with tape.
3. Hold the rod or pencil between the palms of your hands.
4. Rub your hands together to twist the rod or pencil quickly backward and forward. You should see the fish appear in the bowl!

The Happy and Sad Face

1. On a card or piece of white paper, draw the outline of a face with a big grin.
2. Lay a piece of tracing paper over the face and stick it with tape on the left hand side.
3. Trace the face onto the tracing paper but this time give the face a frown instead of a grin.
4. Roll the tracing paper carefully around a pencil.
5. Move the pencil rapidly from left to right, rolling and unrolling the tracing paper as you do so. Watch the expression on the face change from happy to sad. Can you think of other pictures to try this with?

Make Your Own Movie

Equipment: Paper, pencil, needle and thread (or a small notebook).

Find a notebook with small pages or make your own tiny book. To do this, cut the paper into 10 (or more) squares about 3 inches × 3 inches (7.5 cm × 7.5 cm). Fold the pieces of paper in half and stitch the book together along the fold, using a needle and thread. (Ask an adult to help you do this if the paper is rather thick.)

Stitch along the fold.

On each page of the book draw one of the pictures in the sequence to the right. You could make up your own pictures instead so long as each image is only slightly different from the one before. Make sure you draw on only one side of the page. When the book is complete, flick the pages with your thumb and see the story come to life.

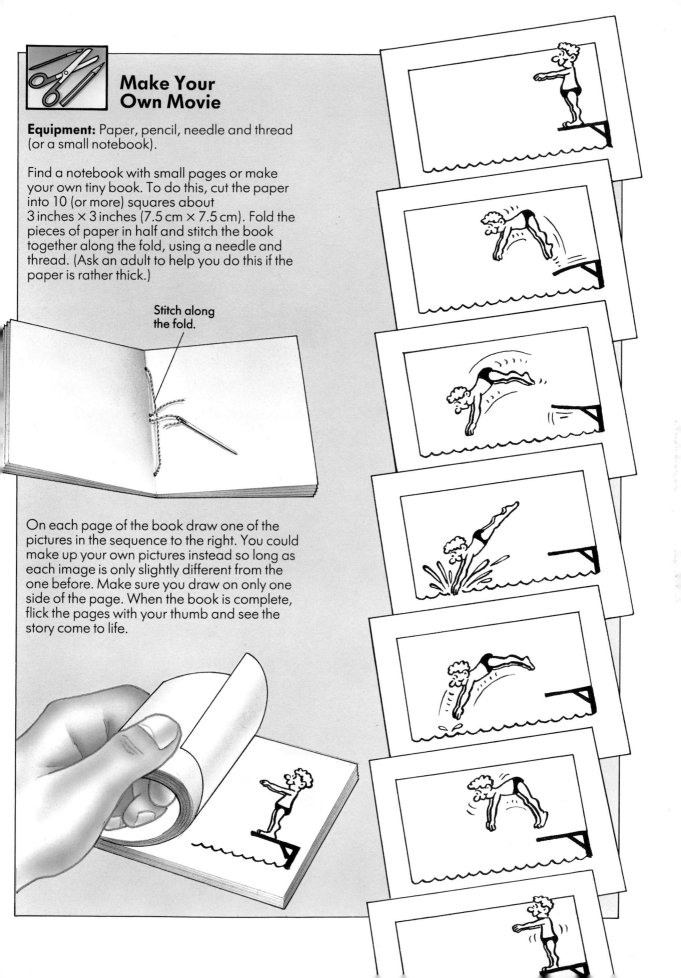

Rainbow Colors

Sunlight or the light from an electric light bulb appears colorless and is called "white light." But it is really made up of a mixture of different colors. We can only see these colors when light passes through a transparent substance (such as water or glass), which separates the colors into a rainbow pattern called a **spectrum**. A spectrum consists of seven colors – red, orange, yellow, green, blue, indigo, and violet – as well as two other kinds of light (ultraviolet and infrared), which we cannot see. You can see a spectrum in bubbles of water or in a rainbow.

Make a Rainbow

A 17th century scientist called Isaac Newton was the first person to show that light can be split up into different colors. He used a small piece of glass with triangular sides (called a **prism**) to do this. You can use a bowl of water and a mirror instead of a prism.

On a sunny day, fill a bowl with water and rest a flat mirror against the inside. Stand the bowl so that sunlight falls onto the mirror. Hold a sheet of white card in front of the mirror and move it around until a rainbow of colors appears on it. You may have to adjust the position of the mirror to get this just right. Once the mirror and card are in the correct position, you can keep the mirror still with a little modeling clay.

How it works
The "wedge" of water between the mirror and the surface of the water acts as a prism and splits up the light so you can see the different colors. This happens because each of the colors in white light travels at a slightly different speed and is bent (refracted – see pages 12–13) inside the prism by a different amount. Violet light bends the most and red light bends the least.

More things to try
Put a magnifying glass between the mirror and the card. You should find that the lens bends the light so the colors come back together again and the rainbow disappears! This shows that the seven colors of the rainbow combine to make white light.

Color Spinners

Here is another way to show that white light is made up of the seven colors of the rainbow.

Equipment: Card, scissors, a short pencil with a sharp point or a pointed stick.

1. Cut out a disk with a diameter of 4 inches (10 cm).
2. Divide it into seven equal sections. Make each section about 51° wide. Use a protractor to divide up the disk.
3. Color each section with one of the colors of the spectrum.
4. Make a small hole in the middle of the disk and push the sharp pencil or stick through.
5. Spin the disk quickly. What do you see?

51°

More things to try
- Make another disk in the same way but divide it into three sections. Color one section red, one blue, and one green. When you spin the disk it will look grayish-white again. This is because red, blue, and green are the main colors our eyes are able to respond to. They are called the **primary colors** of light.
- Try different combinations of two of the primary colors. Make a spinner that is half red and half green and one that is half red and half blue. What colors do you see when you spin the disks? (You will find this is different from mixing colored paints.)

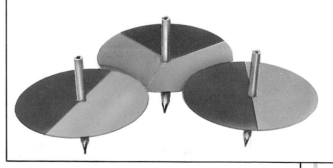

How it works
When the circle spins quickly, your eyes cannot see each color separately. You see only the result of mixing the different colored light together. This is why the disk appears grayish white even though there are really seven colors on it.

What Color is it?

Most objects do not produce light of their own. They reflect the light that falls on them and our eyes see the reflected light. So the color of an object depends on the color of light that it reflects back into our eyes.

► The colors you see depend on the sort of light that falls on objects. Yellow sodium street lights make some colors look very bright. These colors are used in safety equipment and clothing, to make them show up clearly at night.

Explaining Colors

White objects reflect all the colors of light.

Colored objects reflect certain colors and absorb the rest. We see the reflected color. A red shirt looks red because it reflects more of the red part of the spectrum than any other color. It absorbs most of the other colors in the light that shines on it.

Black objects reflect hardly any of the light that falls on them. But even black things reflect some light. The only thing that can be completely black is a hole. Try an experiment to prove this.

Find a box with a lid and cut a small hole in one end of the box. Paint the inside of the box and the surface around the hole black. When you look at the painted surface, it will look black but the hole will seem to be much darker. Any light that goes into the box through the hole bounces from one side of the box to the other. The hole does not reflect any light so it is completely dark.

No Way Through

Most materials reflect all the light that shines on them and do not let any light pass through. They are called **opaque** materials. Some examples are: paper, metal, stone, and cloth.

See-Through Objects

Some materials reflect hardly any light at all. The light passes right through so you can see through them. They are called **transparent** materials. Glass and water are transparent; how many objects made of transparent materials can you think of? (You can find out more about transparent materials on pages 30–31.)

Some Light Gets Through

A few materials reflect some light but also let some light pass through. These are called **translucent** materials. Some examples are: frosted glass, thick plastic, and tracing paper. If you look through a translucent material, things will look blurred.

This is because the light is bent in all directions.

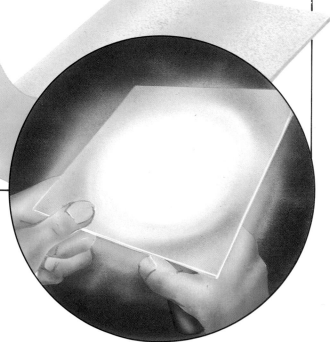

Spot the Difference

You can check to see if an object is translucent or transparent by shining a flashlight behind it in a darkened room. If you can see the light clearly, the object is transparent. If the object looks blurred, the object is translucent.

Changing Color

Transparent materials can be used to make color filters which change the color of the objects that you see through them. A color filter only allows light of its own color to pass through.

Make a Viewing Box

Try this experiment to see what happens to the color of objects when you view them in different colored light.
Equipment: A cardboard box with a lid, colored cellophane, tape, colored objects, scissors.

1. First make color filters. Cut frames from the card about 4 inches × 3 inches (10 cm × 7 cm) in size. Stick a piece of cellophane onto each one.
2. Cut a rectangle out of the lid of the box. (Make it slightly smaller than the frames.)
3. Cut a viewing hole in the side of the box.
4. Place a red cellophane filter over the lid.
5. Put one red object (such as a tomato) and one green object (such as an apple) inside the box. Shine a flashlight through the filter. What color do the objects appear to be when you look through the viewing hole?

How it works
The red filter allows only red light to pass through into the box. The red tomato looks pale because it reflects mainly red light, which can pass through

Turn the World Red

Set up a water prism to make a spectrum on a piece of card (see page 26) or color your own rainbow on a piece of white paper. Look at your rainbow through a piece of red cellophane. What happens to the spectrum?

How it works
You will find that only red light appears on the card. The cellophane is transparent so it lets light pass through it. But it is also red, which means that it absorbs all the colors of the spectrum except red. So only red light shines through onto the card. (The cellophane also reflects some red light so it appears red when you look at it.)

the filter. The green apple reflects mainly green light, which is stopped by the filter. The apple appears dark because there is no light reflected from it. Try looking at the same two objects through a green filter. Does the apple or the tomato look dark this time? Experiment with different colored filters and other objects as well.

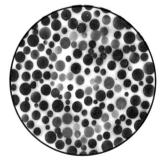

Some people cannot see the difference between red and green. They will not be able to see the letter "S" in the diagram above.

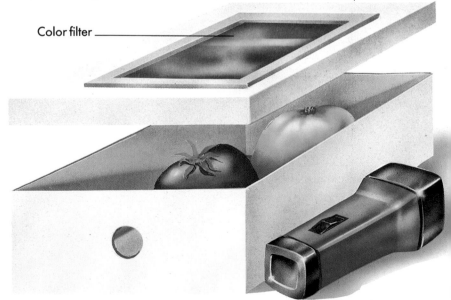

Color filter

▲ Color filters are used to produce spectacular light effects at discotheques.

Make a Stained Glass Window

Stained glass windows also act as color filters. You can make your own with some thin card and colored cellophane or tissue paper.

1. Choose a pattern to put on your window. It can be anything from a rocket to a bumble bee. Draw your design on the card.
2. Decide on your color scheme and mark the different colored areas on the card.
3. Cut out the shapes from the card but remember to leave enough card between the different areas so you can stick the colored cellophane or tissue down.
4. Cut the colored cellophane or tissue to fit behind the holes. Allow a little extra on each piece to stick to the card.
5. Fix the colored shapes on to the card with glue or sticky tape and hang your stained glass window in the light.

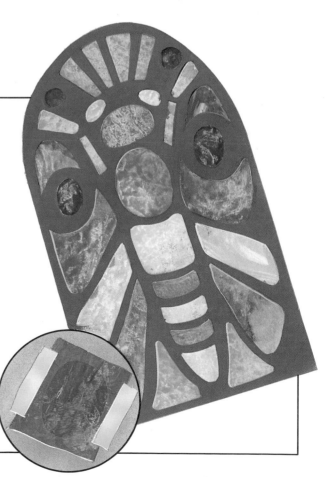

Separating Colors

Colored objects are able to reflect some of the colors in the light that falls on them because they contain substances called **pigments**. You can find out more about pigments by investigating the inks and dyes that people use to color things.

Mixing Paints

Many substances contain several different pigments, which each reflect a different color of light. When you mix paints you are mixing pigments. This does not have the same effect as mixing colored light (see page 27).

Investigating Inks and Dyes

Here is a way for you to separate the different colored pigments in some inks and dyes.
Equipment: White blotting paper (or large coffee filters), a dish or saucer of water, inks or dyes (such as food coloring, felt pens).

1. Cut the blotting paper or filter paper into long strips about 1 inch × 1 foot (2 cm × 30 cm).
2. Put a drop of the ink or dye you want to test about 1½ inches (4 cm) from one end of the paper.
3. Hang the paper strip up so that the end with the drop of ink or dye on it just dips into the saucer of water. You will soon see colored bands spreading up the paper.
4. Take each strip of paper out of the water when the color is nearly at the top. Let the paper dry and you will be able to examine the colors closely.

How it works

The paper soaks up water from the saucer and the water carries the different colors up the paper. The different colored pigments travel at different speeds up the paper so you will be able to see separate bands of color. This is called **chromatography**. Some inks and dyes contain only one color but others are mixtures of two or more colors.

Tie Dyeing

Tie dyeing works by preventing dye reaching some parts of the cloth so that white patterns are left in the colored material.

Equipment: An old handkerchief (or old piece of cloth), string or thread, a cold water dye from a hardware store (or make your own dyes.)

1. Make up the dye according to the instructions.
2. Decide where you would like the patterns to appear on the cloth. Pull a cone of fabric from these areas through your finger or thumb and tie a piece of thread tightly around it. Then tie a second piece of thread or string just below the first one.
3. Complete the dyeing process and then cut the threads.

How it works
The tight threads keep the dye away from the material just below them. These areas stay white and make flower-shaped patterns on the cloth.

Make Your Own Dyes

Long before artificial dyes were invented, people used natural dyes from plants and the soil to color their clothes, pottery, and other objects in their homes. You can try making some dyes for yourself.

Try out the dyes on pieces of white cloth, such as an old handkerchief or squares cut from an old sheet. (Do not use your best shirt as some of the dyes are permanent!) Make sure the cloth is clean and dry. Do not use cloth that has been treated with fabric softeners. These chemicals may stop the dye from working.

Method for Plant Dyes
Boil the leaves or fruit with a little water in a pan. Simmer for about 15 minutes and allow to cool. An alternative method is to put the plant material in a bowl and cover it with boiling water. Leave the bowl for about 15 minutes.

Then make a filter. Cut the top half off a plastic bottle, turn it upside down and put a coffee filter inside. Pour the liquid from the saucepan or bowl through the filter to produce a colored liquid that you can use for dyeing.

Warning: Ask an adult to help you with these experiments as boiling water is dangerous and you might burn yourself. Wear an apron or overall to protect your clothes.

Colors to Try
- **Red** – Beetroot, cherries, red cabbage
- **Yellow** – Onion skins
- **Green** – Spinach
- **Brown** – Iodine, tea, coffee (about 2 teaspoonfuls in half a cup of water).
- **Blue** – Dissolve a spoonful of flour in half a cup of warm water and add one or two drops of iodine.

Light for Life

Green plants need light from the sun to make their food. Without sunlight, green plants will die. Without green plants, all life on earth would be unable to survive. All living things feed on plants or animals that have eaten plants.

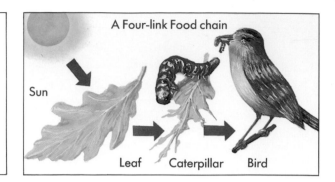

A Four-link Food chain

Sun — Leaf — Caterpillar — Bird

▲ The sun's light energy is trapped by green plants, which are in turn eaten by animals. Food chains link together to form food webs because most animals have several kinds of food.

Plants and Light

Try this experiment to prove that green plants need light to survive.

Find a sheet of cardboard and lay it across a patch of grass. Leave it in place for several days, then lift it up and examine the grass underneath. You will see that the grass looks yellow and unhealthy. If you remove the cardboard after you have finished your experiment, the grass will slowly recover.

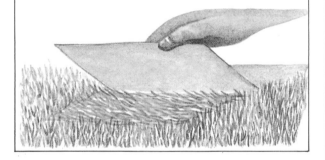

Bow to the Light

Plants grow toward the light so they get as much light as possible. If light is all around them, they grow straight up. If the light comes from one side only, they will grow toward the source of light and bend over. Try growing seeds to see this happen.

Sow some mustard and cress seeds in a little soil on two old saucers. Find a small box with a lid and cut a small hole in one side. Place one saucer in the box and put the lid on. Leave the other saucer in the open. Allow the seeds to grow for about a week. Do they grow differently?

Remember to water the soil if it becomes dry.

Grass grows taller inside "greenhouse."

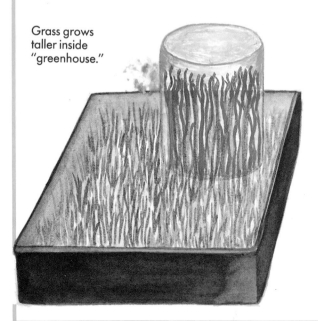

Greenhouses

A greenhouse provides a warm atmosphere for growing plants. Light and heat from the sun passes through the glass and heats up the air inside. This heat cannot escape easily and the air inside stays warmer than the air outside. You can see the effect of a greenhouse by placing a glass jar over a patch of grass or over one section of the seeds growing in a seed tray. Inside your "greenhouse" the plants will grow faster.

Cats' eyes seem to glow in the dark. This is because they have an extra reflective layer at the back of their eyes, behind the retina. At night, when only a small amount of light enters a cat's eyes, the light is reflected back through the retina again. This helps to produce a clear image. Many mammals have this special layer in their eyes; it is called a **tapetum**.

Some animals can produce light. Firefly beetles attract a mate with flashes of light. Different kinds of firefly signal with different patterns of flashes, which helps each individual to recognize others of its own kind.

Some animals use light and color to help them hide from their enemies. This is called **camouflage**. The bush cricket above looks just like a leaf, for example. The stripes on a tiger's body help to break up its outline and make it difficult to see among tall grasses. This helps it to creep up on the animals it hunts without being seen.

Looking at Sunlight

Sunlight contains two types of rays that we cannot see. They are called ultraviolet and infrared rays. The **ultraviolet** rays cause our skin to turn a darker color. The skin darkens to prevent the ultraviolet rays from getting through and damaging the body. Suntan creams contain substances that cut down the amount of ultraviolet light that reaches the skin. The heat of the sun comes from **infrared** rays. These rays can burn the skin if they are too strong.

Heat from the Sun

The heat from the sun warms everything on earth. The land heats up more quickly than the sea but it also cools down more quickly too. You may have noticed that the sea is warmer than the land if you have walked barefoot along a beach in the evening.

1. Fill one of the containers with water and the other with dry soil.

2. Place a thermometer in each container and stand them in a sunny place. Note down the temperature in each container.

Equipment: Two containers, two thermometers, dry soil, water, black cloth.

Soil   Water

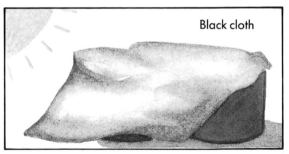

Black cloth

3. Cover the containers with a black cloth and leave them in the sun for about two hours. Note down the temperature every half hour. Which container heats up more quickly? Which one reaches the highest temperature?

4. Now put the two containers in a cool place out of the sun. Which container cools down more quickly?

Bake a Potato

You can use the infrared rays from the sun to cook food and prepare a feast for yourself. Microwave ovens cook food in a similar way.

1. Line the basket with the foil; put the shiny side outward. Make the foil as smooth as possible and tape it in position. (It helps to put a liner under the foil.)
2. Push the nail or fork through the middle of the base of the basket and fix the small potato to it.
3. Set up your "cooker" facing the sun. To get the best results, you should do this on a **very** hot day around noon.
4. Turn the "cooker" to face the sun as it moves across the sky.

How it works
The aluminum foil reflects the sun's rays like a mirror and concentrates them on the potato. The heat warms the potato and should eventually cook it if the sun is hot enough.

Equipment: A small potato, aluminum foil, a round hanging basket frame (and liner if possible) or a round metal bowl, a long nail or fork, sticky tape.

Using Light from the Sun

Solar panels are used in the roofs or sides of buildings to collect heat from the sun. The heat is used to warm rooms and provide hot water. Solar panels are arranged to face the sun for as much of the day as possible. Some kinds can be turned to follow the sun as it moves across the sky. In sunny places, solar panels can be used to provide most of the energy for a home. In other places, they can be used as well as other sources of energy, such as electricity. They are also used on satellites.

Laser Light

Machines called lasers strengthen light energy to produce a narrow beam of light that is amazingly powerful. A laser beam can cut a hole through a steel plate in seconds and can produce a disk of light on the moon. Low-powered lasers are used by doctors to carry out delicate operations. Laser beams also carry signals in video disc players.

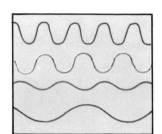

Ordinary (white) light is a mixture of wavelengths (colors) and the waves overlap

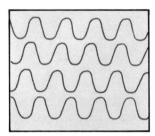

Light of one color is all one wavelength and the waves overlap

A Special Light

Ordinary light from the sun or an electric light bulb is a mixture of different colors. Each color is produced by light of a different wavelength and the waves overlap each other. But in a beam of laser light, the light is only one color so it is all the same wavelength. The waves are also all in step with each other. A laser sends out a narrow beam of light in only one direction and has a lot of energy because it concentrates the light.

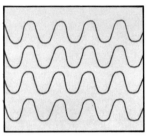

Laser light is all one wavelength and the waves are all in step.

How Lasers Work

Inside a laser is a crystal (such as a ruby) or a tube of gas, (such as carbon dioxide, krypton, or argon). A source of energy (for example a flashing light) directs energy into the crystal or gas. When enough energy has built up, it is released as an intense beam of laser light. The diagram below shows a laser with a ruby crystal inside. This was the first type of laser to be produced.

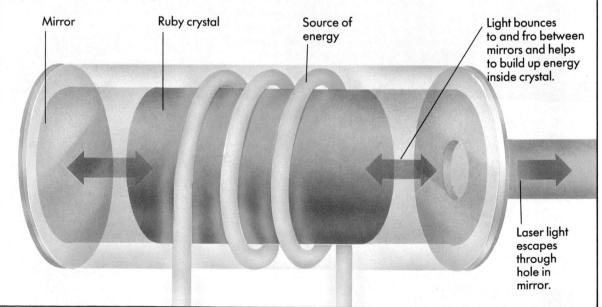

Mirror

Ruby crystal

Source of energy

Light bounces to and fro between mirrors and helps to build up energy inside crystal.

Laser light escapes through hole in mirror.

▲ Laser beams do not spread out like ordinary light beams so they can be used for accurate drilling operations. This laser is being used to drill a hole in aluminum.

◄ Lasers can be used to produce three dimensional pictures called holograms.

Index

Page numbers in *italics* refer to illustrations or where illustrations and text occur on the same page.

Editor: Barbara Taylor
Designer: Ben White
Illustrators: Kuo Kang Chen · Peter Bull
Consultant: Terry Cash

Additional Illustrations: Mike Saunders (*Jillian Burgess*); pages 8–11, 26–33, 38
  Catherine Constable; pages 34–37
  Crocker; pages 19, 25 (Black & white)
Cover Design: The Pinpoint Design Company
Picture Research: Jackie Cookson

Photograph Acknowledgements: 4 top right, 7 ZEFA; 8 top right Nik Cookson; 11 bottom J.Allan Cash; 13 top ZEFA; 14 top Science Museum, London; 17 middle Carl Zeiss Jena Ltd; 28 top right R.O.S.P.A.; 31 top ZEFA; 35 top Nature Photographers, bottom Michael Chinery; 36 top right ZEFA; 39 top Photri, bottom WHO Group.

Published 1987 by Warwick Press, 387 Park Avenue South, New York, New York 10016.

First published in Great Britain by Kingfisher Books Limited.

Copyright © 1987 by Grisewood & Dempsey Ltd.

Printed by South China Printing Company. H.K.
6 5 4 3 2 1
All rights reserved

Library of Congress Catalog Card No. 86-51555
ISBN 0-531-19026-9